ANIMALS AND THEIR HABITATS

Seasonal Forests

WORLD
BOOK

A Scott Fetzer company

Chicago

www.worldbookonline.com

World Book, Inc.
233 N. Michigan Avenue
Chicago, IL 60601
U.S.A.

For information about other World Book publications,
visit our website at http://www.worldbookonline.com
or call 1-800-WORLDBK (967-5325).

For information about sales to schools and libraries, call
1-800-975-3250 (United States), or 1-800-837-5365 (Canada)

Staff

Executive Committee
President: Donald D. Keller
Vice President and Editor in Chief: Paul A. Kobasa
Vice President, Marketing/Digital Products: Sean Klunder
Vice President, International: Richard Flower
Controller: Yan Chen
Director, Human Resources: Bev Ecker

Editorial

Associate Director, Supplementary Publications:
  Scott Thomas
Managing Editor, Supplementary Publications:
  Barbara A. Mayes
Associate Manager, Supplementary Publications:
  Cassie Mayer
Editors: Brian Johnson and Kristina Vaicikonis
Researcher: Annie Brodsky
Editorial Assistant: Ethel Matthews
Manager, Contracts & Compliance
  (Rights & Permissions): Loranne K. Shields
Indexer: David Pofelski
Writer: David Alderton
Project Editor: Sarah Uttridge
Editorial Assistant: Kieron Connolly
Design: Andrew Easton

Graphics and Design

Senior Manager: Tom Evans
Senior Designer: Don Di Sante
Manager, Cartography: Wayne K. Pichler
Senior Cartographer: John Rejba

Pre-Press and Manufacturing

Director: Carma Fazio
Manufacturing Manager: Steven K. Hueppchen
Senior Production Manager: Janice Rossing
Production/Technology Manager: Anne Fritzinger
Proofreader: Emilie Schrage

Library of Congress Cataloging-in-Publication Data

Seasonal forests.
    p. cm. -- (Animals and their habitats)
    Summary: "Text and illustrations introduce readers to
the animals that live in seasonal forests and woodlands
around the world. Detailed captions describe each animal,
while inset maps show where the animals can be found.
Features include a glossary, maps, photographs, and an
index"--Provided by publisher.
    Includes bibliographical references and index.
    ISBN 978-0-7166-0444-0
    1. Forest animals--Juvenile literature. 2. Forest animals--
Habitat--Juvenile literature. 3. Habitat (Ecology)--Juvenile
literature. 4. Seasons--Juvenile literature. I. World Book, Inc.
    QL112.S43 2012
    591.73--dc23
                                          2012005842

Animals and Their Habitats
Set ISBN: 978-0-7166-0441-9

Printed in China by Leo Paper Products., LTD.,
Heshan, Guangdong
1st printing July 2012

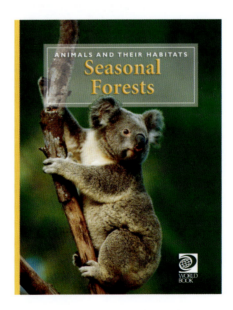

Cover image: The koala, like other
inhabitants of forests that change with
the seasons, is well-suited to the yearly
rhythms of these magnificent ecosystems.
Unfortunately, many creatures that
depend on trees for food and shelter have
become endangered—or even gone
extinct—as forests have been cleared for
farmland or damaged by pollution.

© Horizon International Images
Limited/Alamy

Contents

Introduction 4

Habitat Map 5

Mammals (deer, bears, and their relatives) 6

Amphibians (fire salamander) 38

Insects (ants, beetles, and their relatives) 39

Birds (robins, nightingales, and their relatives) 42

Glossary 46

Resources 47

Acknowledgments 47

Index 48

Introduction

Seasonal forests teem with life. Birds sweep over the treetops. Squirrels and pine martens leap between tree branches. Mighty bears and elk wander through the dappled light falling through the leaves. Ants and beetles work in the soil. Millions upon millions of living things that can be seen only under a microscope also live in the forests.

Seasonal forests are found throughout *temperate* (mild) areas of the world. They stretch across much of Asia, Europe, and North America. They also are found in Australia and South America. Seasonal forests grow beyond the rain forests of the tropics, in areas where the seasons change. Summer gives way to fall, as the leaves of *deciduous trees* (trees that lose their leaves) change color and fall to the ground. In the spring, the trees grow new buds. Other seasonal forests have mainly *conifer trees* (evergreens), which bear cones. Their needlelike leaves shed snow and preserve water in the dry winter air. Conifers do not shed their leaves in winter.

In forests, as in most other *ecosystems*, life depends on energy from the sun. An ecosystem is made up of the plants and animals in an area and their *abiotic* (nonliving or physical) environment, including climate, soil, water, air, *nutrients* (nourishing substances), and energy. Only the green plants in a forest can use the sun's energy directly. Through a process called *photosynthesis*,

STRIPED SKUNK

they use sunlight to produce food. All other forest organisms rely on green plants to capture the energy of sunlight. Some animals, called *herbivores*, eat only green plants. For example, squirrels eat the nuts from trees. They also bury nuts for the winter. Some of these nuts go uneaten and may grow into new trees. In Australia, koalas feed on the leaves of eucalyptus trees. Giant pandas are vegetarian bears that feed on bamboo, a type of woody grass, in forests in China.

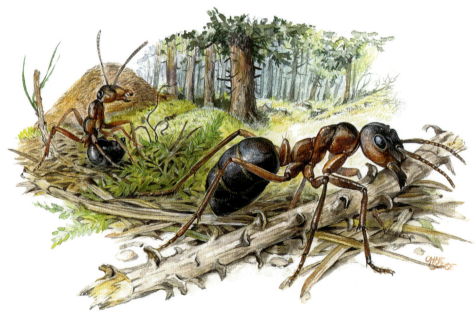

RED WOOD ANT

SEASONAL FORESTS

Other animals, called *predators*, eat herbivores as well as other animals. Wildcats, for example, feed on the many plant-eating rodents that scurry beneath the trees. The kiwis of New Zealand are rare flightless birds. They dig *burrows* (underground shelters) instead of building nests. Unlike most birds, they have a keen sense of smell, which they use to hunt earthworms and insects on the forest floor. Some forest dwellers feed on whatever the forest provides. The striped skunk eats everything from fruit to rodents to animal remains.

Insects and earthworms are vital to the health of the forest. Stag beetles and termites feed on decaying trees, recycling nutrients in the wood. Ants and earthworms turn and enrich the soil, helping plants to grow.

The forest provides little food in the winter. Rodents may *hibernate* (enter a sleep-like state), safe in their burrows. Many forest songbirds *migrate* (travel) to warmer regions ahead of the winter weather. They return the following spring, when insects thrive again on the blooming flowers and plant life.

NORTHERN BROWN KIWI

European Bison

This close relative of the American bison lives mainly in forests rather than in grasslands. It is somewhat smaller than its American cousin, which is also known as a "buffalo."

VITAL STATISTICS

WEIGHT	660–2,020 lb (300–920 kg); males are heavier than females
LENGTH	95–158 in (240–400 cm), including tail
SEXUAL MATURITY	4–6 years; cows mature earlier
LENGTH OF PREGNANCY	Around 280 days
NUMBER OF OFFSPRING	Usually 1 calf, sometimes 2; weaned by 1 year old
DIET	Grazes on vegetation; also browses on leaves and twigs
LIFESPAN	About 15 years; has lived for 28 years in captivity

WHERE IN THE WORLD?

Now present in northern and eastern Europe, extending to Kyrgyzstan and Ukraine.

ANIMAL FACTS

European bison, also called wisents, were once found throughout much of western Asia and Europe. However, hunting and the destruction of their forest *habitat* (living place) caused this bison *species* (kind) to become *extinct* (die out) in the wild by 1927. All of today's surviving population can be traced back to just a dozen survivors that were kept in zoos. Reintroduction programs have since restored the population to about 3,000 individuals. However, the bison remains vulnerable, in part because close relatives are at risk for disease.

Males fight for control of females.

HEAD
The wisent's head is smaller and carried higher than that of the American bison.

HORNS
The horns are more fearsome than those of the American bison.

COAT
The coat is relatively short and less shaggy than that of the American bison.

MUSCULAR BUILD
Well-muscled forequarters help a bison to stand its ground and drive back an opponent.

TAIL
The tail acts as a switch to keep flies away. European bison have longer tails than American bison.

HOW BIG IS IT?

SURVIVING IN SNOW
Bison must eat large amounts of plant foods. In winter, they can dig through snow to find plants beneath, but they often resort to gnawing tree bark.

Roe Deer

SPECIES • *Capreolus capreolus*

These deer are not easy to observe because they are so shy. The male's antlers are lost each autumn and then regrow up to 10 inches (25 centimeters) long the next spring.

VITAL STATISTICS

WEIGHT	40–64 lb (18–29 kg)
LENGTH	40–50 in (101–127 cm), including tail; up to 26 in (67 cm) tall
SEXUAL MATURITY	14 months old
LENGTH OF PREGNANCY	Up to 294 days; weaning occurs at 6–10 weeks, with fawns suckling occasionally through their first winter
NUMBER OF OFFSPRING	1, occasionally 2
DIET	Grazes on grass; browses on leaves and bushes
LIFESPAN	10–14 years

WHERE IN THE WORLD?

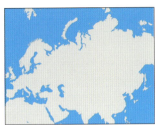

Lives throughout much of Europe and western Asia.

ANIMAL FACTS

These deer are solitary during the summer, with males and females living separately. They come together to mate at the height of summer. The development of the young is delayed so the fawns can be born in the spring. In the winter, the deer live in large family groups. They can feed on about 1,000 kinds of plants, enabling them to survive in many different areas. However, the destruction of forests has reduced their range.

Antler shape changes with age.

COLORATION
This varies through the year, becoming much darker in the winter.

RUMP
This area is white in color, contrasting with the rest of the coat.

EARS
Roe deer have excellent hearing, thanks to their large, mobile ears.

FAWN
Young roe deer have white spots on the back, extending to the flanks.

HOW BIG IS IT?

WINTER SURVIVAL
When there is snow, roe deer may pull down branches to eat, causing damage to forests.

European Elk

VITAL STATISTICS

WEIGHT	Females 600–800 lb (270–360 kg); males 850–1,320 lb (380–600 kg)
LENGTH	95–125 in (240–320 cm), including tail; up to 84 in (213 cm) tall
SEXUAL MATURITY	2–3 years
LENGTH OF PREGNANCY	226–246 days; weaning occurs about 6 months later
NUMBER OF OFFSPRING	1, occasionally twins and rarely triplets
DIET	Grazes on grass; also browses on taller plants
LIFESPAN	8–12 years

ANIMAL FACTS

The European elk belongs to the same species as the North American moose, but the American elk is a different kind of deer. The difference in names amounts to a case of mistaken identity by early European settlers in North America. Almost half of all elk calves die in their first year, mainly because of attacks by wolves and bears. *Predators* (hunting animals) can take down a mature elk only if it is weak or old.

An emerging set of antlers

The European elk is the largest living *species* (kind) of deer. The male's magnificent antlers are carried only until the end of the breeding season, when they fall off. A new pair begins to grow in the spring.

WHERE IN THE WORLD?

Lives in the northern forests of Asia, Europe, and North America.

ANTLERS
The male's antlers have several rounded points. They can stretch up to 72 inches (180 centimeters) wide. The antlers are covered by a protective layer of skin called felt, which is shed after the antlers reach their full size.

SENSES
Elk rely heavily on their senses of smell and hearing. Their eyesight is poor.

VARIATIONS ON A THEME
The antlers change shape at different ages. They may also differ from area to area.

COAT
Hollow hairs in the coat help insulate the elk from the cold.

BELL
A flap of skin and fur, called a bell, hangs from the elk's throat.

HOW BIG IS IT?

A HEALTHY APPETITE

An elk can eat up to 44 pounds (20 kilograms) of vegetation daily. It sometimes grazes on *aquatic* (water) plants.

Sika Deer

VITAL STATISTICS

WEIGHT	65–155 lb (30–70 kg)
LENGTH	45–69 in (115–175 cm), including tail; up to 42 in (110 cm) tall
SEXUAL MATURITY	18 months–2 years
LENGTH OF PREGNANCY	About 220 days; weaning occurs 8–12 months later
NUMBER OF OFFSPRING	1, rarely 2
DIET	Grazes on grass; also browses on taller plants
LIFESPAN	10 years in the wild; up to 20 in captivity

ANIMAL FACTS

Although most deer are relatively quiet, the sika makes at least 10 different calls, including a loud scream. Females live in small groups led by a male. Males are highly territorial and aggressive. They use both their antlers and their sharp hoofs to battle rivals. Both animals can end up being seriously injured in such conflicts. Although Asian sika populations have declined, the deer has been introduced to many countries outside Asia. Hunters prize the sika, partly because its ability to hide makes for a challenging experience.

Some stags live solitary lives.

The word *sika* means *small deer* in Japanese. This deer was once common throughout eastern Asia and Japan, but hunting and the destruction of forests has reduced populations there significantly.

WHERE IN THE WORLD?

Lives in isolated pockets in eastern Asia, from Siberia to China and Korea, and in Japan. It has been introduced to many areas, including Australia, Europe, and the United States.

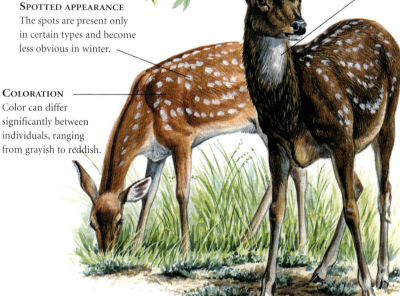

ANTLERS
Present only in males, these can reach 32 inches (81 centimeters) long.

MANE
The coat becomes thicker in winter, creating a mane around the *stag's* (male's) neck.

SPOTTED APPEARANCE
The spots are present only in certain types and become less obvious in winter.

COLORATION
Color can differ significantly between individuals, ranging from grayish to reddish.

HOW BIG IS IT?

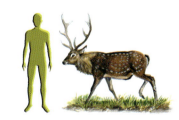

YOUNG SIKA
Fawns are born in May and June. They are at great risk from attacks by wolves.

Indian Muntjac

VITAL STATISTICS

WEIGHT	30–80 lb (14–35 kg)
LENGTH	48–60 in (122–152 cm), including tail; up to 24 in (60 cm) tall
SEXUAL MATURITY	12 months
LENGTH OF PREGNANCY	200–220 days; weaning occurs 2–3 months later
NUMBER OF OFFSPRING	1, rarely 2
DIET	Eats vegetation, fruit, fungi, as well as eggs and animal remains
LIFESPAN	Probably no more than 6 years in the wild, but up to 10 years in captivity

ANIMAL FACTS

The Indian muntjac (*MUHNT jak*) is a shy deer that is active mainly at night. It is hunted by crocodiles, jackals, leopards, pythons, and tigers, among other predators. Upon sensing a predator, the deer may bark for up to an hour. People who hunt pheasants in India have long relied on the muntjac's bark to alert them to the approach of tigers. The deer defends a *territory* (personal space), and adults are solitary except during the breeding season. The young set out on their own after only six months. Numbers of the deer are falling, but it remains common. It can survive even in areas where farming has destroyed its forest *habitat* (living place).

This animal is also known as the barking deer, for the dog-like barks it makes when threatened. Although it is small, its fierce temperament can make it a hard catch for *predators* (hunting animals).

WHERE IN THE WORLD?

Lives in India and Southeast Asia, extending north as far as southern China, south to the Indonesian islands of Java and Sumatra, and east to Borneo.

BONY RIDGES
These ridges, seen in both sexes, are the bases from which the male's antlers grow.

ANTLERS
These are present only in the male. They reach 6 inches (15 centimeters) in length.

CANINE TEETH
The male's upper *canines* (biting teeth) form small tusks, up to 1 inch (2.5 centimeters) long.

GLANDS (ORGANS)
So-called "tear glands" are found in front of the eyes. These produce a scent used to mark the deer's territory.

HOW BIG IS IT?

SOUND THE ALARM

Muntjacs are hunted by tigers and other predators. The deer bark mainly to harass predators, to let them know that any chance for an ambush has already been lost.

Siberian Musk Deer

VITAL STATISTICS

WEIGHT	24–40 lb (11–18 kg)
LENGTH	35–42 in (90–106 cm), including tail; up to 22 in (55 cm) tall
SEXUAL MATURITY	Females 4–10 years; males 7–12 years
LENGTH OF PREGNANCY	About 200 days; weaning occurs 3–4 months later
NUMBER OF OFFSPRING	Usually 2, sometimes 3
DIET	Grazes on grass and lichens; also browses on taller plants
LIFESPAN	10–14 years; up to 20 in captivity

ANIMAL FACTS

This animal is among the most primitive *species* (kind) of deer. They lack antlers and grow long *canines* (biting teeth). The deer live in mountain forests. They are generally solitary and active at night. Females give birth in the early summer. Fawns hide until they are about eight weeks old. Males make a powerful musk, which is highly valued for perfume. The deer is endangered because of *poaching* (illegal hunting) to harvest the musk.

The deer browses on high plants, especially when snow covers the ground.

These graceful deer run quickly and can leap more than 16 feet (5 meters) in a single bound. When threatened, they head for rocky terrain and try to reach an inaccessible crag.

WHERE IN THE WORLD?

Extends through central Asia to northern Mongolia and China, south to Korea.

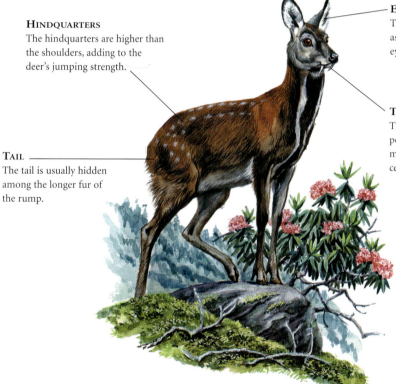

HINDQUARTERS
The hindquarters are higher than the shoulders, adding to the deer's jumping strength.

TAIL
The tail is usually hidden among the longer fur of the rump.

EARS AND EYES
The ears are broad and tall as well as mobile, and the eyes are large.

TEETH
The protruding, backward-pointing upper canines can measure up to 4 inches (10 centimeters) long.

HOW BIG IS IT?

COVERED IN SPOTS

Fawns are heavily spotted on their upperparts until they are about 18 months old. The spots help to keep them concealed in a sun-dappled forest, protecting them from *predators* (hunting animals).

Wild Boar

VITAL STATISTICS

WEIGHT	100–700 lb (45–320 kg); males are heavier than females
LENGTH	40–95 in (105–240 cm), including tail; up to 45 in (110 cm) tall
SEXUAL MATURITY	Around 18 months
LENGTH OF PREGNANCY	112–130 days; weaning occurs 3–4 months later
NUMBER OF OFFSPRING	Usually 4–8, but can be up to 13
DIET	Eats fruit, roots, grain; also small animals, eggs, and animal remains
LIFESPAN	Can be up to 21 years

This animal is the wild relative of the *domesticated* (tamed) pig. Wild boar has been prized by hunters for centuries, partly because the sharp tusks and ferocity of these beasts make them dangerous game.

WHERE IN THE WORLD?

Ranges across parts of Europe and much of southwestern and central Asia. Also lives in parts of North Africa.

ANIMAL FACTS

The wild boar is active mainly from dusk until dawn. Smell is by far the animal's most important sense. They often dig up the soil to find food, helping to promote new plant growth. Males fight for access to *sows* (females) during the breeding season. Their sharp tusks can cause great damage. Domestic pigs have much less hair, usually pink skin, and shorter tusks.

TUSKS
These teeth extend beyond the lips and serve as deadly weapons.

COAT
The coat is coarse, with a bristly texture. It is brownish in young animals but becomes more gray with age.

LEGS
The legs are long and well-muscled, giving the boar great strength. The animal even swims well.

Boar (above) and sow (below).

HOW BIG IS IT?

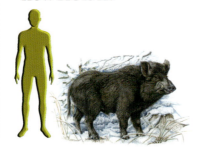

WALLOWING IN MUD
Wallowing in mud helps the wild boar to stay cool in the summer. It also protects against sunburn and insect bites.

Collared Peccary

VITAL STATISTICS

WEIGHT	31–68 lb (14–31 kg); males are heavier
LENGTH	32–43 in (82–110 cm), including tail; up to 20 in (50 cm) tall
SEXUAL MATURITY	Females 8–14 months; males 11–12 months
LENGTH OF PREGNANCY	141–151 days
NUMBER OF OFFSPRING	1–5
DIET	Eats fruit, roots, and other plant matter; also animal remains
LIFESPAN	Up to 24 years

ANIMAL FACTS

Peccaries live in herds that usually have 5 to 15 members. The herd does almost everything together. It is led by the largest male. Peccaries mark their *territory* (space) with oily *musk* (strong smelling substance) and droppings. Members of the herd drive away strange peccaries that enter their territory. They charge and bite to fight off the intruders. Peccaries have poor eyesight but sharp senses of smell and hearing. They communicate with a variety of calls. Females give birth on their own, but mother and young rejoin the herd the following day.

Beady eyes suggest poor eyesight.

Peccaries are often called "javelinas" because their sharp tusks are said to resemble the throwing spears known as javelins. They are also called "musk hogs," a reference to their strong odor.

WHERE IN THE WORLD?

Lives in the southern United States, through Central America, and east of the Andes down to northern Argentina and Brazil in South America.

MUSK
Glands (organs) on the back release an oily, smelly fluid that the animals use to mark their territory.

HEAD
The head is narrow and ends in a flexible snout. The ears are small.

BODY
The body is rounded, with the tail barely visible.

COAT
The coat of bristly hair is grayish to grizzled black, with a yellow neck band.

HOW BIG IS IT?

SUCKLING
Young peccaries nurse for two to three months. Unlike the adults, the young are yellowish brown with a black stripe down the back.

European Wildcat

VITAL STATISTICS

WEIGHT	6.5–17.5 lb (3–8 kg)
LENGTH	30–54 in (75–138 cm), including tail; about 16 in (40 cm) tall
SEXUAL MATURITY	6–12 months
LENGTH OF PREGNANCY	63–68 days
NUMBER OF OFFSPRING	Average 2–4, but can be up to 8; weaning at around 80 days
DIET	Hunts small prey, mostly rodents
LIFESPAN	8–10 years, although can live up to 15

The house cat beloved by pet owners was domesticated from wildcats in Africa as long as 5,000 years ago. The shy European wildcat is a *subspecies* (variety) of wildcat that lives in the forests of Europe.

WHERE IN THE WORLD?

Lives in forested areas in the Iberian Peninsula and along the Mediterranean, to Turkey and the Caucasus. An isolated population lives in Scotland.

ANIMAL FACTS

The European wildcat is extremely shy and hides well in the forest. It often hunts at night. It hunts mainly rodents, though it also catches birds. It has keen eyesight and hearing. Unfortunately, the European wildcat is now highly endangered. Threats include loss of its forest *habitat* (living place), poisoning, and being hit by cars. But the biggest threat to the animal's survival is mating with *domestic* (tamed) cats. There are so many domestic cats that the unique traits of wildcats will disappear if breeding between the two continues.

A dog that chases a wildcat may be in for a nasty surprise involving claws.

COLORATION
Coat color is variable, from slate gray to dark brown, with tabby markings. —

TAIL —
The tail is usually shorter and thicker than that of a domestic cat.

HEAD
The head is broad with powerful jaws. White fur may extend from around the jaws down the throat.

FEET
There are only four toes here, with all the cat's claws protected by sheaths.

HOW BIG IS IT?

RUNNING WILD

A domestic cat (right, top) compared with a European wildcat (right, bottom). The wildcat is usually larger and stronger than its domestic relative. It also lives alone and is difficult to approach.

Ocelot

VITAL STATISTICS

WEIGHT	25–35 lb (11.5–16 kg)
LENGTH	3.5–4 ft (107–120 cm), including tail
SEXUAL MATURITY	2 years
LENGTH OF PREGNANCY	79–85 days
NUMBER OF OFFSPRING	2–4
DIET	Rodents, rabbits, snakes, lizards, birds, young deer, and monkeys
LIFESPAN	Probably 5–7 years in the wild

ANIMAL FACTS

Ocelots are difficult to observe in the wild because they are shy and active mostly at night. During the day, they usually sleep in trees or hide in thick vegetation. The cats are solitary and territorial, with a male's *territory* (space) over-lapping those of several females. Kittens become independent after a year. These cats were once heavily hunted for their beautiful fur. They are now protected by law, but they remain *threatened* (in danger of dying out) by *poaching* (illegal hunting) and loss of forests.

Ocelots can haul themselves up a tree using their sharp claws.

The ocelot is a graceful climber, partly because it has large, strong paws. In fact, it is often called the *manigordo,* which is Spanish for *big feet.* The cat spends much of its time in trees.

WHERE IN THE WORLD?

Found in far southern parts of the United States, across Central America, down through South America to northern Argentina, east of the Andes.

BODY PATTERN
These body markings provide *camouflage* (disguise) in sun-dappled forests.

EYES AND EARS
The large eyes and ears provide the cat with keen vision and hearing even at night.

UNDERPARTS
The background color on the underparts of the body is usually paler than the flanks.

HUNTING HABITS
Ocelots hunt their prey in the trees, on the ground, and even in water. Rodents are their preferred prey.

HOW BIG IS IT?

Eurasian Badger

VITAL STATISTICS

WEIGHT	18–26 lb (8–12 kg)
LENGTH	35 in (90 cm)
SEXUAL MATURITY	12–15 months
LENGTH OF PREGNANCY	42–56 days; development can be delayed for up to 10 months after fertilization
NUMBER OF OFFSPRING	Average 2–3, ranges from 1–6; weaning at 12–20 weeks
DIET	Feeds mainly on worms; also insects, rabbits, nuts, fruit, and other plant matter
LIFESPAN	3–15 years; 19 in captivity

ANIMAL FACTS

A badger's sett, or *burrow* (underground shelter), may be occupied by many generations of Eurasian badgers, each of which enlarges the area. Some setts may be more than 100 years old. The badgers are territorial, and each territory usually has more than one sett. The badgers emerge as night falls, to search for food. In spite of their peaceful appearance, badgers are aggressive if cornered. They are capable of inflicting serious injuries with their teeth and claws. Their young are born in late winter. They first venture out of the sett at 2 months old.

Badgers rely on their rugged claws for digging and to catch prey.

Eurasian badgers live in groups known as clans, with about six adults and their offspring. They shelter in a network of underground tunnels and in larger chambers that are called setts.

WHERE IN THE WORLD?

Extends from Spain, across Europe into Asia, reaching as far east as China and Japan.

COLORATION
Mostly gray on the upperparts and black on the underside.

STRIPING
Black and white stripes extend from the head along the sides of the face to the neck.

LEGS
Like other burrowing animals, badgers have short but powerful legs, with rugged claws.

HOW BIG IS IT?

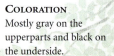

TUNNELING AWAY
A badger sett is an amazing piece of engineering. The entrances often are surrounded by bare soil.

Striped Skunk

VITAL STATISTICS

WEIGHT	3–10 lb (1.4–4.5 kg)
LENGTH	20–28 in (51–71 cm), including tail; up to (10 in) 25 cm tall
SEXUAL MATURITY	About 2 years
LENGTH OF PREGNANCY	42–63 days
NUMBER OF OFFSPRING	5–6; weaning at around 42 days
DIET	Eats insects, rodents, eggs, birds, fish, fruit, nuts, plant matter, and animal remains
LIFESPAN	6–8 years in the wild; up to 15 in captivity

Skunks spray a foul-smelling liquid when threatened. The spray comes from a pair of *glands* (organs) near the base of the skunk's tail.

WHERE IN THE WORLD?

Lives widely across North America, extending from the southern half of Canada across the United States to Mexico.

ANIMAL FACTS

The skunk depends on its *musk* (foul-smelling substance) for protection, partly because its short legs do not enable it to run quickly. If threatened, the skunk gives warning by stamping its front feet and by hissing or growling. If this fails, it will spray. In addition to its foul odor, the spray stings painfully if it enters the eyes. In most cases, the spray buys the skunk enough time to escape to the safety of its *burrow* (underground shelter). Skunks can spray accurately at targets up to 12 feet (3.7 meters) away.

A striped skunk sprays a mountain lion.

PATTERNING
Broad white stripes run down each side of the body from the head; the central area is black.

TAIL
The tail is bushy, with a blend of white and black fur.

LEGS
The short legs end in webbed toes, equipped with rugged claws.

HEAD
The head is triangular and covered with short hair, with a white stripe between the eyes.

NOT A PICKY EATER
The skunk eats a variety of food, depending on the season and availability of plants and small animals.

HOW BIG IS IT?

Northern Raccoon

VITAL STATISTICS

WEIGHT	9–20 lb (4–9 kg); males are heavier
LENGTH	24–42 in (61–107 cm); about 12 in (30 cm) tall
SEXUAL MATURITY	Females 2 years; males 3 years
LENGTH OF PREGNANCY	54–70 days; typically 65 days
NUMBER OF OFFSPRING	2–5, averages 4; weaning occurs at 16 weeks
DIET	Eats crabs, frogs, fish, mice, insects, worms, eggs, corn, fruits, seeds, and other plant matter
LIFESPAN	2–3 years; up to 16 years in captivity

ANIMAL FACTS

Raccoons *adapt* (adjust) to different foods and environments, including cities. This flexibility has enabled them to thrive even as people have cut down their forest *habitat* (living place). Many people believe that raccoons wash their food before they eat it, but this is not so. Raccoons in zoos often dunk their food, but they are apparently imitating the way wild raccoons catch food in streams. Raccoons carry rabies and other diseases, so people should not approach them.

The hind feet are longer and narrower than the front feet.

Raccoons are curious by nature, and their hand-like paws enable them to lift lids and even open latches. As a result, they often raid garbage cans and may even invade homes.

WHERE IN THE WORLD?

Extends from Canada through the United States into Central America, as far south as Panama. Introduced to parts of Europe and Asia.

EARS
The ears are edged with white fur. The raccoon has sharp hearing.

FACIAL COLORING
The black fur around the eyes is often described as a "bandit's mask."

LEGS
Raccoons are strong climbers and usually climb trees if they feel threatened.

TAIL
The tail is long, with alternating dark and white rings down its length.

OUT OF TROUBLE
A female raccoon rears the young—called kits—on her own, sometimes carrying them by the scruff of the neck.

HOW BIG IS IT?

Pine Marten

SPECIES • *Martes martes*

Graceful yet fierce, the pine marten is a great hunter of the trees, leaping from branch to branch after squirrels. Trees also offer cover from birds of prey, which feed on these animals.

VITAL STATISTICS

WEIGHT	1–4.5 lb (0.5–2.2 kg); males are heavier
LENGTH	18–21 in (46–54 cm); up to 6 in (15 cm) tall
SEXUAL MATURITY	2–3 years
LENGTH OF PREGNANCY	31 days; development starts about 7 months after fertilization
NUMBER OF OFFSPRING	2–3; weaning occurs at around 49 days
DIET	Hunts a wide variety of small animals, especially rodents; also eats fruit
LIFESPAN	6–8 years; up to 18 in captivity

ANIMAL FACTS

The pine marten is active mainly at night. During the day, it nests in hollow trees or abandoned squirrel or bird nests. The animal feeds mainly on squirrels and other rodents but eats a variety of foods. In the past, pine marten numbers fell because of trapping for their valuable pelts. Today, the animal has recovered in many areas, though it remains *threatened* (in danger) by the loss of its forest *habitat* (living place).

Pine martens usually sleep off the ground.

WHERE IN THE WORLD?

Ranges across Europe into western Asia, down to parts of the Middle East.

HEAD
The pine martin has triangular ears, prominent whiskers, and a narrow, pointed muzzle.

CHEST
The bib, or upper chest, has a creamy-yellow color.

PAWS
The fur on the paws is a darker shade of brown than on the body.

HEADING DOWN
The pine marten's sharp claws help this animal maintain its grip when it is climbing trees in the forest.

HOW BIG IS IT?

FUR
The fur becomes darker and silkier in the winter. It was once highly prized for use in clothing.

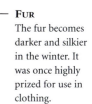

WINTER WALKING
The undersides of the pine marten's toes are protected by fur in the winter, helping it to walk comfortably over snow.

Red Panda

VITAL STATISTICS

WEIGHT	9–13 lb (4–6 kg)
LENGTH	24 in (61 cm), including tail
SEXUAL MATURITY	About 18 months
LENGTH OF PREGNANCY	112–158 days
NUMBER OF OFFSPRING	1–5, but averaging 2
DIET	Feeds mainly on bamboo; also other vegetation, bird eggs, and chicks
LIFESPAN	12–14 years

Scientists debated this animal's origins for years. Many grouped the red panda and the giant panda with raccoons. However, research has shown that the red panda is not closely related to any living species.

WHERE IN THE WORLD?

Found in the Himalayan region, through southern Asia, from Nepal through Bhutan and northern Myanmar (also known as Burma) to China.

ANIMAL FACTS

Red pandas live mainly in trees. Much of the day is spent asleep or foraging for food. When resting, red pandas curl up and wrap their tails around themselves, often hiding in a tree hollow. They eat mainly bamboo, grasping it between their fingers and an "extra thumb." This thumb is actually a bone that grows from the wrist, covered by a fleshy pad. The pandas also have true thumbs, which they use as fingers. The destruction of bamboo forests has left these animals *threatened* (in danger of dying out). Only about 10,000 red pandas are thought to remain in the wild.

COLORATION
The fur is a rich russet color, with black legs and underparts.

STANDING TALL
These pandas can stand up on their hind legs.

EARS
The ears are broad and pointed, whitish in color, and set low on the head.

FACIAL MARKINGS
Brown stripes extend below the eyes; the muzzle is white.

TAIL
The tail is thick and well-furred, with lighter rings along its length.

The claws only partially retract.

HOW BIG IS IT?

GROUND LEVEL
It is usually only at night that red pandas leave the trees to roam on the ground, where they move more slowly.

Giant Panda

The giant panda is a most unusual bear that feeds almost exclusively on bamboo. Only about 2,500 of these majestic animals are thought to survive in the wild.

VITAL STATISTICS

WEIGHT	220–330 lb (100–150 kg); males are heavier
LENGTH	About 63 in (160 cm); about 30 in (75 cm) tall
SEXUAL MATURITY	4–8 years
LENGTH OF PREGNANCY	95–160 days
NUMBER OF OFFSPRING	1–2; weaning occurs at about 1 year
DIET	Feeds on bamboo; rarely feeds on small animals
LIFESPAN	20–30 years

WHERE IN THE WORLD?

Restricted to southwestern parts of China.

ANIMAL FACTS

Bamboo is abundant, but the giant panda must eat vast quantities to meet its needs. It is not able to draw much energy from plants, unlike such animals as cattle. The giant panda tends to move slowly, to save energy. It is territorial and usually solitary. Unlike other bears, it does not *hibernate* (enter a sleep-like state) or shelter in dens in the winter. Instead, it moves to lower elevations. The giant panda is threatened mainly by the destruction of bamboo forests. The Chinese government has established a system of nature reserves to protect these animals.

Territorial marking includes spraying urine and leaving scratch marks on trees.

MATERNAL INSTINCTS

Newborn giant pandas may weigh only about 3 ounces (90 grams). They spend nearly seven hours a day nursing.

HOW BIG IS IT?

MARKINGS
The eyes are surrounded by black fur.

FRONT PAWS
Like the red panda, the giant panda has an "extra thumb" that enables it to grasp bamboo.

COAT
The coat is thick and woolly, protecting against the cold.

Brown Bear

VITAL STATISTICS

WEIGHT	215–500 lb (97–226 kg); males are heavier
LENGTH	70–115 in (180–293 cm); about 59 in (150 cm) tall
SEXUAL MATURITY	5–7 years; males may not breed until 10
LENGTH OF PREGNANCY	186–248 days; development begins 5 months after fertilization
NUMBER OF OFFSPRING	1–5, averages 2; weaning occurs at 6–8 months
DIET	Eats fruits and other plant matter; also a variety of small animals
LIFESPAN	Up to 30 years; 40 in captivity

ANIMAL FACTS

Brown bears have *adapted* (adjusted) to many foods and *habitats* (living places). They are usually solitary, but they do not defend a territory. In the winter, the bear *hibernates* (enters a sleep-like state). It shelters in a den, usually one it has dug in the soil. The young are born blind and hairless. Cubs usually remain with their mother for three or four years. Brown bears remain numerous, but they have been killed off in many areas of Asia, Europe, and the United States.

The claws are formidable.

The brown bear is a strong and fearsome *predator* (hunting animal). It can outrun a horse and kill an elk with one mighty blow. However, many brown bears have been killed by human beings.

WHERE IN THE WORLD?

Lives in northwestern parts of North America, across northern Europe and Asia. Also present in some areas of Asia farther south.

HUMP
This distinctive feature is made of muscle.

EYES
These are small and provide relatively weak eyesight, but the bear has a keen sense of smell.

COLORATION
Despite their name, brown bears can vary from shades of blond through brown to black.

CLAWS
These are used for digging and also climbing. They can reach about 6 inches (15 centimeters) long.

HOW BIG IS IT?

ESCAPE FROM HARM
Young bears will flee up a tree if they detect danger. A mother with cubs can be dangerous to people. But brown bears usually avoid human beings.

Grizzly Bear

VITAL STATISTICS

WEIGHT	400–600 lb (180–275 kg); males are heavier
LENGTH	71–84 in (180–213 cm) overall; about 59 in (150 cm) tall
SEXUAL MATURITY	5–7 years; males may not breed until 10
LENGTH OF PREGNANCY	186–248 days; development begins 5 months after fertilization
NUMBER OF OFFSPRING	2, ranges from 1–5; weaning occurs at 6–8 months
DIET	Eats nuts, fruit, leaves, and roots; also a variety of mammals, salmon, and animal remains
LIFESPAN	Up to 30 years

The grizzly bear is a larger *subspecies* (variety) of brown bear. Its name comes from the grayish or "grizzled" hairtips of adults. For the same reason, grizzly bears are sometimes called silvertips.

WHERE IN THE WORLD?

Lives in northwestern North America, mostly in Alaska and Canada, though small numbers survive in Wyoming, Montana, and Idaho.

ANIMAL FACTS

Grizzlies are usually solitary, except when they gather to feast on salmon. At this time, a grizzly can eat up to 90 pounds (40 kilograms) of food a day. By eating so much, the bear builds up fat. The fat enables the bear to *hibernate* (enter a sleep-like state) in the winter. Despite their size, grizzlies can run at speeds of 37 miles (60 kilometers) per hour. They also swim well.

THE SENSES
Broad, wide nostrils give these bears a keen sense of smell, but their eyes are relatively small.

FOREQUARTERS
These are immensely powerful, with legs that are thick and strong.

SIZE
Grizzlies living in the far north are typically larger than those farther south.

COLORATION
The bear's grayish flecking accounts for its name.

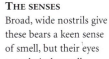

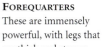

Grizzlies may mark their *territory* (personal area) by making scratches on a tree.

NATURE'S BOUNTY

Grizzlies may feast on salmon that swim upstream to reproduce. Young bears need time to learn how to fish well.

Paw prints reveal the powerful claws.

HOW BIG IS IT?

Bank Vole

VITAL STATISTICS

WEIGHT	0.6–0.7 oz (17–20 g)
LENGTH	4 in (10 cm)
SEXUAL MATURITY	4–5 weeks
LENGTH OF PREGNANCY	18–20 days; 3–6 litters a year
NUMBER OF OFFSPRING	3–5; weaning occurs at around 3 weeks
DIET	Leaves, buds, flowers, fungi, nuts, and insects
LIFESPAN	Up to 18 months

ANIMAL FACTS

Bank voles are eaten by birds of prey, foxes, snakes, weasels, and many other animals. Without these predators, bank voles would soon become so numerous that they would do great damage to plants. In fact, many voles die of starvation in the winter, when food is hard to find. As a result, most bank voles live less than a year. Both male and female voles are territorial. The *territory* (personal area) of a male usually overlaps those of several females. Pups are born blind and helpless in an underground nest. The nest is usually lined with grass. The mothers care for the newborns. She weans her pups in less than a month and may soon be pregnant with her next litter.

Bank voles can breed at a rapid pace, producing several litters a year. However, their numbers are usually kept in check by *predators* (hunting animals).

WHERE IN THE WORLD?

Found across much of Europe, extending to western Asia.

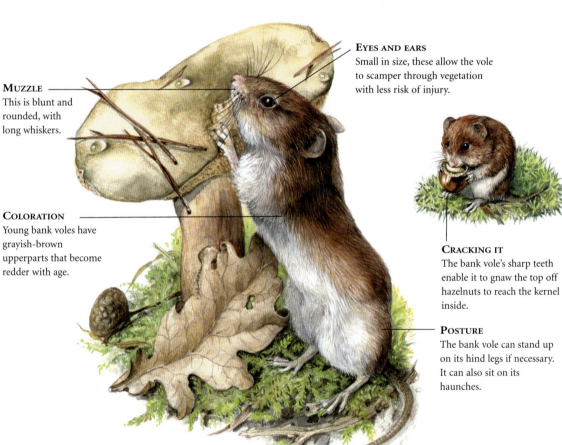

MUZZLE
This is blunt and rounded, with long whiskers.

COLORATION
Young bank voles have grayish-brown upperparts that become redder with age.

EYES AND EARS
Small in size, these allow the vole to scamper through vegetation with less risk of injury.

CRACKING IT
The bank vole's sharp teeth enable it to gnaw the top off hazelnuts to reach the kernel inside.

POSTURE
The bank vole can stand up on its hind legs if necessary. It can also sit on its haunches.

HOW BIG IS IT?

PREPARING FOR WINTER
Bank voles often collect and store food during the fall, so that they have something to eat when snow blankets the ground.

Common Dormouse

VITAL STATISTICS

WEIGHT	0.5–1 oz (15–30 g); males slightly bigger
LENGTH	About 6 in (16 cm) long, including tail
SEXUAL MATURITY	Around 12 months
LENGTH OF PREGNANCY	Around 19 days
NUMBER OF OFFSPRING	2–7, typically 6; weaning occurs at 36–40 days; young disperse at 10 weeks
DIET	Flowers and pollen in the spring; fruit and nuts over the summer
LIFESPAN	Around 2.5 years

ANIMAL FACTS

Dormice feed in the trees, relying on their grace and speed to leap among the branches. There they are hunted by falcons and other birds. From late summer through fall, they build up fat to sustain themselves over the winter. They hibernate in *burrows* (underground shelters) dug into the soil. Their body temperature falls nearly to freezing, and they appear dead. They recover in the spring, having lost much of their body weight. During hibernation, they may be dug up and eaten by red foxes and wild boars.

The dormouse's name comes from the French word *dormir*, meaning *to sleep*. Dormice *hibernate* (enter a sleep-like state) for seven months each year.

WHERE IN THE WORLD?

Found across much of Europe, except for the west and far north, extending into western Asia.

EYES
These are relatively large, as is typical of an animal that is active at night.

FEET
These enable the dormouse to walk along even narrow twigs.

TAIL
The long tail is covered with fur, right to the tip.

COLORATION
Golden-brown fur over the back and sides of the body, and pale cream underparts.

HAZELNUTS
Bitemarks on hazelnuts can indicate the presence of dormice. Squirrels split the nuts to obtain the kernel, but dormice create a small hole and remove it in pieces.

HOW BIG IS IT?

BREEDING
To raise their young, dormice make ball-shaped nests of dry grass, usually among the tree branches.

Eurasian Red Squirrel

SPECIES • *Sciurus vulgaris*

VITAL STATISTICS

WEIGHT	About 20 oz (600 g)
LENGTH	13–17 in (34–43 cm), including tail
SEXUAL MATURITY	11 months
LENGTH OF PREGNANCY	38 days; 2 litters a year
NUMBER OF OFFSPRING	3–6; young eat solid food from 40 days, but may suckle for 10 weeks
DIET	Nuts, seeds, berries, shoots, insects, and bird eggs
LIFESPAN	Up to 7 years

ANIMAL FACTS

The red squirrel is a graceful climber and can escape danger in the trees. However, the trees do not offer protection from pine martens. The squirrel remains active in the winter, relying on food it buries in the ground. Although it remains numerous overall, the red squirrel has disappeared from some areas, including southeastern parts of the United Kingdom. It suffers from a loss of forest, but even more, from competition with the eastern gray squirrel, which was introduced from North America.

Summer coat (top) and darker winter coat (bottom).

Despite their name, red squirrels may be brown or even black. These rodents prefer to live in large, mature trees with holes in the trunk, where the squirrels can build their nests.

WHERE IN THE WORLD?

Found in northern parts of Europe, extending to the Pacific coast of Asia.

COLORATION
Vibrant red coats are most common in the population found in the British Isles.

EAR TUFTS
These are much larger in the winter, as part of the animal's warm winter coat.

TEETH
Their sharp *incisor* (biting) teeth allow these squirrels to extract seeds easily from pine cones.

HOW BIG IS IT?

JUMPING
The powerful hind legs of these squirrels help them to leap from one branch to another.

North American Porcupine

SPECIES • *Erethizon dorsatum*

This porcupine is the second-largest rodent in North America, rivaled only by the beaver. It lives in woodland areas, where it often climbs trees in search of food. Its body is protected by about 30,000 quills.

VITAL STATISTICS

WEIGHT	10–40 lb (4.5–18 kg)
LENGTH	12–48 in (30–122 cm); quills 3 in (7.5 cm) long on average
SEXUAL MATURITY	Females 25 months; males 29 months
LENGTH OF PREGNANCY	205–217 days; quills harden after birth
NUMBER OF OFFSPRING	1–2; weaning occurs at 4–5 months
DIET	Leaves, twigs, and shoots in summer; gnaws through bark to reach soft wood in winter
LIFESPAN	5–6 years; 18 in captivity

WHERE IN THE WORLD?

Widely distributed across northern North America, from Alaska to Mexico, extending to the northeastern United States.

ANIMAL FACTS

Quills are actually hollow hairs that are *fused* (grown together). They have sharp *barbs* (points) on the end. The quills detach easily, and the barbs draw the quills deeper into an attacker's flesh. The quills may even kill *predators* (hunting animals) by causing infection. Porcupines are usually solitary, though several may share a *burrow* (underground shelter) in the winter. Both males and females defend *territories* (personal areas). Males fight for access to females.

The porcupine's feet, with five toes on each hindfoot, help them maintain their grip when climbing.

QUILLS
When the porcupine is at rest, these stiff, sharp bristles are kept flat against the body. When it is threatened, it raises its quills.

TEETH
There is a broad muzzle with powerful *incisor* (biting) teeth.

LEGS
These are short, with powerful claws to help the porcupine climb.

TAIL
Unlike many mammals that live in trees, porcupines have relatively short tails.

HOW BIG IS IT?

DEFENSIVE STRATEGY
Few animals can follow porcupines into the trees. Those that do may come away with a face full of quills.

Rhesus Monkey

VITAL STATISTICS

WEIGHT	12–25 lb (5.5–12 kg); males are heavier
LENGTH	18–25 in (46–64 cm)
SEXUAL MATURITY	Females 3–4 years; males around 6–8 years
LENGTH OF PREGNANCY	About 165 days
NUMBER OF OFFSPRING	1; weaning occurs from 4 months
DIET	Eats mainly fruit, leaves, seeds, nuts, roots, and bark; also insects and small animals
LIFESPAN	Probably 10–15 years; can be up to 30 in captivity

ANIMAL FACTS

Rhesus monkeys live in groups called troops, with up to 100 members. The troops are noisy and active. They are not territorial, and different troops may share an area where food is abundant. In India, rhesus monkeys are common in cities, where they may damage gardens. However, the monkeys are sacred to Hindus, so people often tolerate them. As research animals, rhesus monkeys helped scientists understand blood types, among many other discoveries.

Body language is important to rhesus monkeys: staring at another individual and revealing the teeth are threats.

The rhesus monkey grows well in captivity, and it suffers many of the same diseases as human beings. As a result, it has long been an important research animal.

WHERE IN THE WORLD?

Ranges across southern Asia, from Afghanistan to Thailand, up to northern China.

TAIL
The tail is relatively short because these monkeys spend most of their time on the ground.

APPEARANCE
The fur is mostly brown. The monkey usually walks on all fours.

SWIMMING
Rhesus monkeys swim well, so they are able to cross stretches of water in search of food.

OFFSPRING
Offspring ride on their mothers for months after birth. Females provide most care for young.

FACIAL PATTERNING
The fur on the face is short, emphasizing the monkeys' expressions. The ears are conspicuous.

HOW BIG IS IT?

GROOMING
Mutual *grooming* (cleaning) reinforces bonds between troop members and gives them opportunities to remove ticks and other parasites.

Noctule Bat

VITAL STATISTICS

WEIGHT	0.7–1.5 oz (19–40 g)
LENGTH	2.4–3.1 in (6–8 cm); wingspan up to 18 in (45 cm)
SEXUAL MATURITY	10 months–2 years; males mature earlier
LENGTH OF PREGNANCY	About 49 days; mating takes place in fall but development does not occur until spring
NUMBER OF OFFSPRING	1–2; weaning at 42–49 days
DIET	Hunts insects, mainly moths, lacewings, and beetles
LIFESPAN	Up to 12 years

ANIMAL FACTS

Noctule bats hunt flying insects, mostly in the evening and before dawn. They use sounds to track insects in the dark. They also call with sharp cries or trilling similar to birdsong. Like many other bats, noctules usually *hibernate* (enter a sleep-like state) in the winter. Many thousands travel to caves, where they hang from the ceiling for months. During the summer, several hundred bats may *roost* (perch) together in trees, flying off to hunt as the sun sets.

While hibernating, noctule bats may not feed for nearly four months.

These woodland bats are the largest bat *species* (kind) in Europe. The bat is the only *mammal* (animal that feeds its young on the mother's milk) capable of powered flight, though some others are able to glide.

WHERE IN THE WORLD?

Lives throughout much of Europe, across Asia to Japan, south into Vietnam and Singapore.

WINGS
The wings are pointed and narrow; helping the bats to fly fast, at speeds that reach up to 30 miles (50 kilometers) per hour.

SKIN COLOR
The nose, ears, and wings are dark brown.

COLORATION
Golden-brown overall, but paler on the underside of the body.

EARS
These are large and set low on the head.

ON THE TRAIL

Noctule bats hunt by means of sounds too high in pitch for people to hear, an ability called *echolocation*. The difference in the returning sound waves allows the bat to track the position of insects and avoid obstacles in its path. Echolocation enables bats to hunt in darkness.

HOW BIG IS IT?

Nine-Banded Armadillo

VITAL STATISTICS

WEIGHT	9–20 lb (4–8 kg); males are heavier
LENGTH	2–2.6 ft (60–80 cm)
SEXUAL MATURITY	6–12 months
LENGTH OF PREGNANCY	120 days; mating occurs in summer; development begins 3 months later
NUMBER OF OFFSPRING	Usually 4; weaning begins at 4–5 months
DIET	Eats mainly insects and other small animals; also some plants
LIFESPAN	Up to 15 years

Unlike most mammals, armadillos have little body hair to provide warmth. As a result, they live only in warm areas and shelter in *burrows* (underground shelters) even in relatively mild, cool weather.

WHERE IN THE WORLD?

Ranges across the southern parts of the United States, through Central America to South America, as far as Peru and Uruguay. Also present in the Caribbean.

ANIMAL FACTS

The bony plates that cover the armadillo provide hard but flexible armor. This armor protects the animal from most *predators* (hunting animals). The softer armor of the young makes them vulnerable to alligators, bobcats, coyotes, wolves, and others. Armadillos dig several burrows using their strong claws. They usually give birth to four young at once. The young are always identical, because they develop from a single egg. Armadillos can carry disease.

ARMORED BODY
Different *species* (kinds) of armadillos have different numbers of bands around the middle of the body. This armadillo— the most widespread kind—has nine bands, with shields across the rump and shoulders.

HIND FEET
Of the five toes on each foot, the outer ones are shorter.

FRONT FEET
The middle two of the four toes on each foot are the longest.

FACIAL SHAPE
The face is long, with sensitive nostrils and a sticky tongue to catch insects.

Nine-banded armadillos use their strong claws for digging.

HOW BIG IS IT?

ARMADILLO BANDS
The number of bands can range from three to nine. The armadillo's body armor extends over the forehead.

Common Hedgehog

SPECIES • *Erinaceus europaeus*

The flexible snout of this *insectivore* (insect eater), combined with its snuffling behavior when sniffing around for food, helps explain why it became known as the hedgehog.

VITAL STATISTICS

WEIGHT	1.5–2.5 lb (0.8–1.2 kg)
LENGTH	5–9 in (12–23 cm)
SEXUAL MATURITY	1 year
LENGTH OF PREGNANCY	35 days; females may produce 2 litters a year
NUMBER OF OFFSPRING	1–9, typically 5; weaning occurs after 35 days
DIET	Eats mainly insects but also snails, worms, bird eggs, and even small snakes
LIFESPAN	Up to 8 years in the wild; 10 years in captivity

ANIMAL FACTS

Hedgehogs are solitary and active at night. As a result, people most often see them out on summer evenings after rainfall, when their prey is also active. In late summer, they start to put on weight to *hibernate* (enter a sleep-like state) through the winter. The animal's *spines* (stiff, needle-like growths) protect it from most *predators* (hunting animals). However, some animals have learned to drop hedgehogs from a height, stunning them long enough for the predator to attack.

Rolling into a ball protects the hedgehog's vulnerable head and underparts from attack.

WHERE IN THE WORLD?

Found across most of western Europe, including southern Scandinavia, and east into parts of Russia. It was introduced to New Zealand in the 1800's.

SPINES
There are several thousand spines covering the upperparts.

SENSES
Hedgehogs have poor eyesight but keen hearing and smell.

UNDERPARTS
The underparts are covered in dark hair.

GRABBING A MEAL
The hedgehog's sharp teeth help it to grab prey, with the *incisors* (biting teeth) at the front of the mouth serving as fangs.

HOW BIG IS IT?

Tasmanian Devil

VITAL STATISTICS

WEIGHT	9–25 lb (4–12 kg); males are heavier
LENGTH	32–35 in (81–90 cm)
SEXUAL MATURITY	2 years
LENGTH OF PREGNANCY	21 days; the tiny young mature in the mother's pouch
NUMBER OF OFFSPRING	20–30; most die due to lack of food; survivors leave the pouch at around 100 days old
DIET	Mostly animal remains; also small mammals
LIFESPAN	Up to 8 years

ANIMAL FACTS

A rare cancer threatens to wipe out these highly *endangered* (at risk of dying out) marsupials. Cancer usually cannot spread from one creature to another. However, Tasmanian devils are all closely related. As a result, the cancer spreads when the animals bite one another, which is an ordinary part of their courtship. The cancer causes tumors to develop around and inside the mouth, causing infected animals to starve to death. Only about 10,000 devils are thought to remain in the wild.

The Tasmanian devil has sharp teeth and often bites other devils during the breeding season.

These animals get their name from their fierce displays, which include harsh screeches and snarls. They are *marsupials* (a type of mammal that gives birth to tiny young that develop in the mother's pouch).

WHERE IN THE WORLD?

Found only on the island of Tasmania, off Australia's southeastern coast.

TAIL
This stores fat, so a thin tail may indicate poor health.

WHISKERS
The whiskers help the animal sense its surroundings in the dark.

FRONT LEGS
The front legs are longer than the hind legs, which is unusual among marsupials.

NIGHT HUNTER
Tasmanian devils hide away during the day. They hunt at night.

HOW BIG IS IT?

FIGHTING

Fighting is common among Tasmanian devils during the breeding season. They often carry scars for life.

Virginia Opossum

VITAL STATISTICS

WEIGHT	9–13 lb (4–6 kg)
LENGTH	2.5 ft (76 cm), including tail
SEXUAL MATURITY	By 1 year
LENGTH OF PREGNANCY	13 days; young stay in their mother's pouch for 1–2 months
NUMBER OF OFFSPRING	6–25; weaning occurs from 3 months
DIET	Eats a wide variety of foods, including insects and other small animals, animal remains; also some plants
LIFESPAN	2–4 years

ANIMAL FACTS

Opossums are *marsupials* (animals that carry their developing young in a pouch). The female gives birth after only 13 days. The tiny young then crawl to the safety of their mother's pouch, where they continue to grow. If threatened, opossums can growl and bare their teeth. But there is little they can do to defend themselves. As a result, they may play dead instead. Cats and other *predators* (hunting animals) often lose interest in an animal if they think it is already dead. Thus, the phrase "playing possum" means pretending to be dead.

Playing dead or "possum" can cause a predator to lose interest in the opossum.

The ancestors of this animal arrived in North America from South America about 3 million years ago. Although they are similar in many ways, the *opossums* of the Americas are not closely related to the *possums* of Australia.

WHERE IN THE WORLD?

Lives in parts of southern Canada, through the United States east of the Rocky Mountains, along the west coast, down into Mexico and Central America.

FUR
The fur varies in color from shades of gray through to black.

FACIAL FEATURES
Opossums have a narrow snout, with a pink nose and large whiskers.

TAIL
This can grasp branches, helping the animal to support itself off the ground.

TEETH
The mouth has a formidable array of some 50 small, sharp teeth.

HOW BIG IS IT?

POSTURE
Opossums can walk on all fours along a branch, and then sit up and support themselves on their hindquarters.

Whiptail Wallaby

SPECIES • *Macropus parryi*

VITAL STATISTICS

WEIGHT	15–57 lb (7–26 kg); males are bigger
LENGTH	59–77 in (150–195 cm), including tail, which is almost as long as the body
SEXUAL MATURITY	Females 18 months–2 years; males 2 years
LENGTH OF PREGNANCY	34–38 days; weighs 0.03 oz (1 g) at birth
NUMBER OF OFFSPRING	1; the *joey* (young) spends around 275 days in the pouch
DIET	Grasses, ferns, herbs
LIFESPAN	Up to 14 years

ANIMAL FACTS

Wallabies are similar to kangaroos in most respects, though they are smaller. The whiptail wallaby lives in upland wooded areas of Australia. It faces few dangers, other than attacks by *dingoes* (wild dogs). Like kangaroos, wallabies are *marsupials* (animals that carry their young in a pouch). When the young are born, they weigh only about as much as a paper clip. They spend nearly nine months in their mother's pouch, drinking milk to grow. By contrast, human beings and most other mammals are *placentals*. Placental mammals develop inside the mother's body for months and do not grow further inside a pouch. Whiptail wallabies have been kept as pets and are said to behave much like dogs.

This wallaby lives in groups called "mobs" that may have up to 80 members. It is also called the pretty-faced wallaby, because of its distinct white cheeks.

WHERE IN THE WORLD?

Common in eastern Australia.

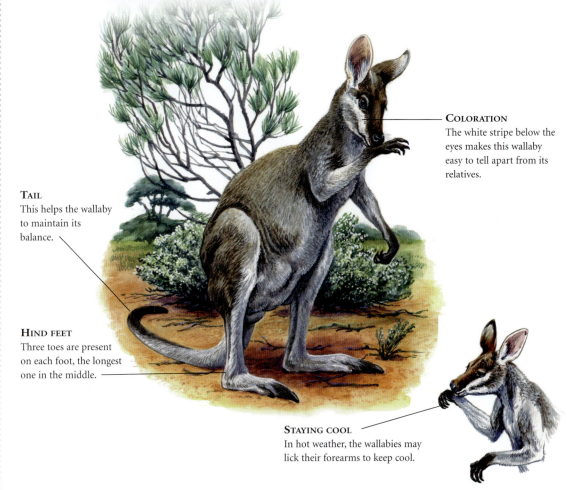

COLORATION
The white stripe below the eyes makes this wallaby easy to tell apart from its relatives.

TAIL
This helps the wallaby to maintain its balance.

HIND FEET
Three toes are present on each foot, the longest one in the middle.

STAYING COOL
In hot weather, the wallabies may lick their forearms to keep cool.

HOW BIG IS IT?

ON THE MOVE

Wallabies rely on their strong hind legs to propel themselves along by long leaps, with both legs moving together.

Koala

VITAL STATISTICS

WEIGHT	15–30 lb (7–14 kg); males are bigger
LENGTH	25–30 in (64–76 cm)
SEXUAL MATURITY	Females 2–3 years; males 3–4 years
LENGTH OF PREGNANCY	34–36 days; newborn koalas measure 0.8 in (2 cm) and weigh under 0.03 oz (1 g)
NUMBER OF OFFSPRING	1; young spend about 215 days in the pouch
DIET	Eucalyptus leaves
LIFESPAN	12 years

ANIMAL FACTS

The leaves of eucalyptus trees contain *toxins* (poisons) that kill most animals, but *microbes* (organisms) in the koala's gut break down the toxins. However, the leaves provide relatively little energy, so the koala moves slowly. The strong odor of eucalyptus makes the koala smell a bit like a cough drop. Koalas were hunted nearly to *extinction* (death) in the early 1900's, mainly for their fur. Today, koalas are protected by law, but their numbers are falling because of disease and the loss of their forest *habitat* (living place).

Although twin births are rare, the female's pouch can support two offspring at a time.

The koala is often called a bear, but it is not related to bears. Instead, it is another *marsupial* (animal that carries its young in a pouch). It is among the few animals that can feed on the leaves of eucalyptus trees.

WHERE IN THE WORLD?

Common in eastern Australia, they have been introduced to parts of western Australia and some offshore islands.

OFFSPRING
After leaving the pouch, a young koala is carried on its mother's back.

SIZE
Those koalas living farther south, where the weather is cooler, are the largest in size.

NOSE
The black nose is prominent, with downward-facing nostrils.

FOREFEET
The presence of *opposable thumbs* makes it easier for koalas to climb and grip branches. (An opposable thumb can be moved against the fingers.)

HOLDING ON
The opposable thumbs on the hind feet help the koala to maintain its grip while it feeds.

HOW BIG IS IT?

SAFE IN THE TREETOPS
Although they usually move slowly, koalas are graceful when they leap among the treetops. They are at risk only when they come to the ground.

Common Wombat

VITAL STATISTICS

WEIGHT	30–100 lb (15–54 kg); males are slightly larger
LENGTH	25–50 in (67–130 cm); the tail is 1 in (2.5 cm) long
SEXUAL MATURITY	Typically 2–3 years
LENGTH OF PREGNANCY	20–22 days
NUMBER OF OFFSPRING	1; young spend six months or more in the pouch
DIET	Eats grass, leaves, bark, and fungi
LIFESPAN	5–15 years in the wild; up to 26 in captivity

ANIMAL FACTS

The common wombat is solitary and active at night. During the day, it shelters in a large *warren* (ground filled with bur-rows). Although wombats remain common, numbers have fallen. Wombats are eaten by *dingoes* (wild dogs) and struck by cars. It also faces competition from rabbits, which were introduced to Australia in the 1800's. The northern hairy-nosed wombat, a close relative of the common wombat, is highly *endangered* (at risk of dying out). Scientists have discovered fossils of a ancient wombat that reached the size of a hippo. It became extinct about 50,000 years ago.

The female's pouch opens at the rear of the body. The young may emerge after six months.

The common wombat is an Australian *marsupial* (animal that carries its young in a pouch). It spends much of its time sheltering in a *burrow* (underground structure), emerging at night to feed on plants.

WHERE IN THE WORLD?

Found in southeastern Australia and Tasmania.

EARS
The triangular ears are small and relatively inconspicuous.

HEAD
This is rounded and broad, ending in a large black nose, surrounded by whiskers.

FUR
The texture is coarse to the touch, with softer insulating fur beneath.

COLORATION
Color is variable, ranging from black and shades of gray through brown to a sandy color.

USEFUL TOOLS
Strong claws help the wombat dig.

WELCOME TO THE WARREN
Warrens may have long tunnels and several chambers.

HOW BIG IS IT?

Short-Beaked Echidna

SPECIES • *Tachyglossus aculeatus*

Echidnas are extremely unusual among mammals in that they give birth by laying eggs. Egg-laying mammals are known as *monotremes*. The echidna and platypus are the only monotremes that still exist.

VITAL STATISTICS

WEIGHT	7–22 lb (3.2–10 kg)
LENGTH	12–18 in (30–45 cm)
SEXUAL MATURITY	5 years, but breeding does not occur for several years more
INCUBATION PERIOD	Egg develops in the body for 21–28 days, and is incubated by the female, hatching 10 days later
NUMBER OF OFFSPRING	1; weaning occurs at 6 months
DIET	Eats ants, termites, and other insects
LIFESPAN	Up to 45 years

WHERE IN THE WORLD?

Found throughout Australia and Tasmania.

ANIMAL FACTS

The echidna sweeps up ants and other insects with its sticky tongue. The female carries her egg in a pouch on her underside. After hatching, the youngster, called a *puggle*, stays in the pouch for several weeks. It is then reared in a *burrow* (underground shelter). The puggle nurses for more than half a year. Unlike other mammals, monotremes lack nipples. Instead, a patch of skin secretes milk. The milk is pink because it is high in iron. The milk is so rich that the female can leave her puggle alone for up to 10 days after a feeding.

The echidna can defend itself with its spurs or roll into a ball.

SNOUT
The snout measures 3 inches (7.5 centimeters), with the tiny mouth at the end only opening to 0.2 inch (0.5 centimeter).

BODY COVERING
The fur between the sharp spines helps to keep the body warm.

SPINES
Many sharp spines jut from the echidna's back and sides. For this reason, the animal is also known as "the spiny anteater."

LIMBS
Short limbs equipped with strong claws enable the echidna to bury itself quickly when threatened.

SPURS
Males have spurs on their hind legs. Unlike platypus spurs, the spurs of the echidna do not carry *venom* (poison).

HOW BIG IS IT?

DISAPPEARING UNDERGROUND

The underside of the body is covered by fur, so echidnas dig quickly to escape danger.

Fire Salamander

VITAL STATISTICS

LENGTH	Typically 6–10 in (15–25 cm); males are smaller
SEXUAL MATURITY	4–5 years
NUMBER OF OFFSPRING	Up to 70
HABITAT	Damp areas, of woodland
DIET	Eats insects, worms, snails, and other small animals
LIFESPAN	Up to about 20 years

The black and orange-yellow markings of these amphibians serve as warning coloration. They signal to *predators* (hunting animals) that the skin of the salamander is *venomous* (poisonous).

WHERE IN THE WORLD?

Ranges across much of southern and central Europe, to the western shores of the Black Sea.

ANIMAL FACTS

The fire salamander is a shy *amphibian* (cold-blooded animal) that is active mainly at night. During the day, it hides under logs or rocks. It requires a moist *habitat* (living place), or its moist skin will dry out. The fire salamander's skin tastes bad, so most predators will spit it out even before they are poisoned. In addition, the salamander can spray its poison at predators to discourage attack. The salamander's eggs develop inside the female's body. After the eggs hatch, the mother gives birth to *larvae* (young) that resemble tadpoles. The larvae mature in water, where they go through a *metamorphosis* (transformation) to become adults. The adults typically spend most of their time on land. The number of these salamanders is falling, mostly because of damage to the environment.

TAIL
Similar in length to the body, the tail has a rounded tip.

POISON GLANDS
Glands (organs) in the skin produce venom that can sicken predators.

TOES
The toes are rounded and stubby.

LEGS
These salamanders can run to cover quickly, but they are not strong climbers.

HOW BIG IS IT?

TO EACH HIS OWN
No two fire salamanders are identical in appearance. The yellow-orange spots and lines form different patterns.

Red Wood Ant

SPECIES • *Formica polyctena*

VITAL STATISTICS

LENGTH	Workers 0.6–0.8 in (1–1.5 cm); queen is larger
NUMBER OF EGGS	Over her lifetime, one queen can lay millions
DEVELOPMENTAL STAGES	Eggs hatch into *larvae* (grubs), which form *pupae* (an inactive stage), and then adults
HABITAT	Forest floor
DIET	Eats insects and other small animals
LIFESPAN	Queens live for 5 years, workers for a few weeks

ANIMAL FACTS

Ants are *eusocial* (*yoo SOH shuhl*) insects. Such insects live in colonies led by a *queen* (egg-laying female). Only the queen reproduces. Nearly all of her offspring are females that work for the benefit of the colony. These ants are called workers. Workers raise the young, gather food, and defend the colony's nest. The nest can be more than 3 feet (0.9 meter) high and 7 feet (2 meters) across. Worker ants defend the nest with ferocity. In addition to using their large jaws and stingers, workers can squirt acid on invaders, dissolving their outer shell.

Worker ants fight to defend their nest against other ants.

Nests of these insects can hold more than 500,000 ants. These ants improve the health of the forest, because their tunnels help to bring air, *nutrients* (nourishing substances), and water down into the soil.

WHERE IN THE WORLD?

Lives in Europe and Asia, with its range extending up to the forests of Scandinavia, south to the Mediterranean and east into Russia.

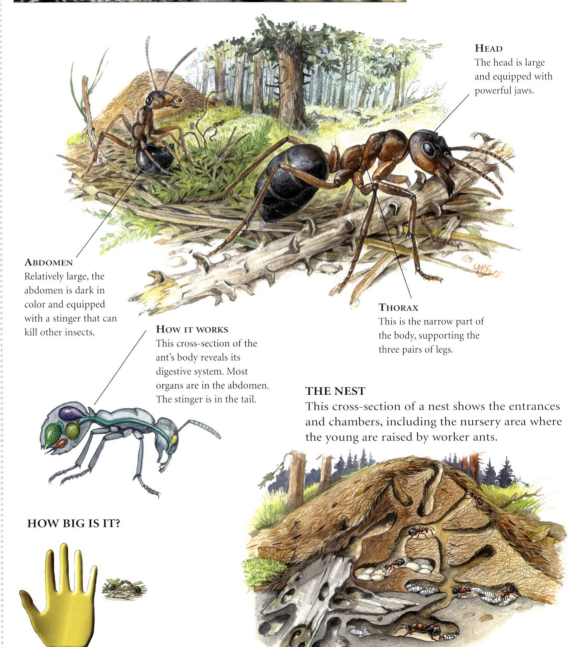

HEAD
The head is large and equipped with powerful jaws.

ABDOMEN
Relatively large, the abdomen is dark in color and equipped with a stinger that can kill other insects.

HOW IT WORKS
This cross-section of the ant's body reveals its digestive system. Most organs are in the abdomen. The stinger is in the tail.

THORAX
This is the narrow part of the body, supporting the three pairs of legs.

THE NEST
This cross-section of a nest shows the entrances and chambers, including the nursery area where the young are raised by worker ants.

HOW BIG IS IT?

Burying Beetle

VITAL STATISTICS

LENGTH	1–2 in (2.5–4.5 cm)
NUMBER OF EGGS	1–30, laid near animal remains
DEVELOPMENT PERIOD	Young mature after a week; life cycle takes 45–60 days
HABITAT	Woodlands and grasslands
DIET	Remains of small mammals and birds
LIFESPAN	Up to 1 year

These insects are also known as "gravedigging beetles." As this name suggests, the beetles bury dead animals, providing their young with a feast of flesh.

WHERE IN THE WORLD?

Widespread in warm and seasonal areas of Asia, Europe, North America, and South America.

ANIMAL FACTS

These beetles can home in on animal *carcasses* (remains) using their keen sense of smell. In fact, they can detect a corpse 2 miles (3.2 kilometers) away. A number of beetles may be drawn to the body. They usually fight until a pair remains to claim possession of the carcass. After the body is buried, female lays her eggs near the remains. When the *larvae* (young) hatch, they can feed themselves, but they are also fed by the adults. Burying beetles provide an important service to the forest by recycling *nutrients* (nourishing substances) locked up in animal remains. Their waste returns nutrients to the soil. In this way, they help plants to grow. The North American burying beetle has become highly *endangered* (at risk of dying out). Loss of forests and other *habitat* (living place) destruction has greatly reduced this beetle's range.

ANTENNAE
These are mainly used to sense odors, enabling the beetle to find a rotting corpse.

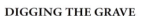

CARCASS
The beetle feeds on the carcasses of rodents and birds.

DIGGING THE GRAVE

The beetles bury the dead animal to prevent it from being taken by other *scavengers* (animals that eat dead animals).

1. The beetles spray the body with liquids that slow the rate of decay and mask the smell.

2. The body is rolled into a ball in the ground. The entire burial process takes about eight hours. Then the fur or feathers are stripped off.

3. The eggs are laid near the body in a chamber called the crypt. They hatch after a few days, and the young strip the flesh from the body.

4. If there are too many young for the available food, the parents kill some to ensure the survival of the rest.

INSECT COLOGNE
To attract a mate, the male releases a scent called a pheromone (*FEHR uh mohn*).

PATTERNING
Orange-red markings are set against a black background.

HOW BIG IS IT?

1.   2.   3.

Stag Beetle

VITAL STATISTICS

LENGTH	Males up to 3 in (7 cm) from the tip of the horn to the end of the abdomen; females average 1.5 in (3.5 cm)
NUMBER OF EGGS	12–24, hatching after 3 weeks
DEVELOPMENT PERIOD	Lifecycle lasts 4–7 years
DIET	Decaying wood and plant matter; adults feed on nectar and tree sap
LIFESPAN	Adults live for about 4 months

ANIMAL FACTS

Stag beetles spend most of their lives as *larvae* (grubs) that live in tree stumps and decaying wood. They feed on the wood and decaying leaves. It is only at the end of their lives that they go through a *metamorphosis* (transformation). The adults live only a few months. Their main purpose is to mate. Adults take to the air on calm summer evenings in search of mates. These flights put them at risk of being eaten by bats and birds. Adults die after the breeding season. These beetles are in decline because of loss of forests.

A comparison between the head of the male (left) and female (right).

The male stag beetle has large "antlers," explaining the beetle's name. Males lock their antlers together and engage in contests of strength. The victor wins access to females.

WHERE IN THE WORLD?

Present across Europe, east to Greece, Turkey, and Syria.

COLORATION
Appears blackish, with a purplish hue.

MOUTHPARTS
Without antlers in the way, the female's jaws can inflict a painful bite.

ANTLERS
Males wrestle each other by locking their antlers, which have points like those of stags.

HEAD SHAPE
The head of the male stag beetle is broad, to allow for the span of the antlers.

BORING TOGETHER

Up to 50 grubs may be present in a single tree stump. They form a distinctive C-shape and are blind.

HOW BIG IS IT?

Willow Tit

VITAL STATISTICS

WEIGHT	0.4 oz (12 g)
LENGTH	4.7 in (12 cm)
WINGSPAN	7.5 in (19 cm)
SEXUAL MATURITY	1 year
INCUBATION PERIOD	14 days
FLEDGLING PERIOD	17–20 days
NUMBER OF EGGS	6–8 eggs
NUMBER OF BROODS	1 a year
TYPICAL DIET	Insects and other small animals in the summer; seeds and berries in the winter
LIFESPAN	Up to 10 years

ANIMAL FACTS

The willow tit makes its nest inside soft or decaying trees, which are much easier to hollow out than a healthy tree. The bird prefers mature forests, especially those with birch, willow, and alder trees. The nest is usually lined with gathered fur, hair, and wood chips. The willow tit makes a *tchay-tchay-tchay* call, and it sings *pee-oo pee-oo*. It usually does not *migrate* (travel) with the seasons, remaining in the same area its entire life.

Willow tits typically nest inside decaying trees.

This bird was immortalized by Gilbert and Sullivan's famous comic opera *The Mikado* (1885), which featured the song "Willow Titwillow Titwillow" about a lovelorn songbird.

WHERE IN THE WORLD?

Found across much of Europe and northern Asia.

EYES
The eyes are set on opposite sides of the head, helping the bird to watch for danger.

COLORATION
Grayish coloration helps the bird to blend in with the pale bark of birch, willow, and alder trees.

FEET
The feet are well suited to grasping branches, like those of other perching birds.

HOW BIG IS IT?

CHISEL BILL

The bill of a bird reveals how it feeds. Willow tits have short bills that serve as chisels to probe bark for insect grubs. The bill is also well suited for pecking insects or seeds off the ground.

European Robin

SPECIES • *Erithacus rubecula*

VITAL STATISTICS

WEIGHT	0.6–0.8 oz (16–22 g)
LENGTH	5 in (14 cm)
SEXUAL MATURITY	Breeds in the year after hatching
NUMBER OF EGGS	3–9, white to shades of pale blue with reddish spotting
INCUBATION PERIOD	12–15 days; the young fledge by 15 days, and the adult pair may breed 2–3 times annually
DIET	Earthworms and insects; also eats seeds, especially in winter
LIFESPAN	Up to 8.5 years but usually less

This bird has long been associated with Christmas in Europe, a tradition that may have arisen because of its cheery winter song. The name "robin" is used for many birds with orange or reddish breasts.

WHERE IN THE WORLD?

Lives throughout most of Europe, east to Iran and the Caucasus, across the Mediterranean to western North Africa.

ANIMAL FACTS

The robin is a common sight in gardens, where it often shows its bold nature. The bird will not hesitate to dart in and pick up a worm dug up from the soil. Robins are watchful birds, and their keen eyesight helps them detect insects and worms on the move. People also encounter these birds in forests, their natural home. Robins usually do not *migrate* (travel) with the seasons, but those that live in northern forests fly south for the winter.

Robins will venture into shallow water to catch small fish.

BILL
Slender and long, the bill is ideal for picking up seeds, turning leaves, and seizing insects.

LOW DOWN
Robins spend much of their time close to the ground, often concealed in undergrowth.

RED BREAST
This is present in both sexes. Males and females are nearly identical.

MOVEMENT
Robins hop along on the ground rather than walk, like many perching birds.

TOUCHING DOWN
The robin uses its wings as brakes to slow its descent, adopting an almost vertical position and extending its legs forward for landing.

HOW BIG IS IT?

Nightingale

VITAL STATISTICS

WEIGHT	0.6–0.8 oz (17–23 g)
LENGTH	6 in (16 cm)
SEXUAL MATURITY	Breeds in the year after hatching
NUMBER OF EGGS	4–5, white to shades of pale blue with reddish spotting
INCUBATION PERIOD	13–15 days; the young fledge by 13 days, and the adult pair may breed 1–2 times annually
DIET	Feeds largely on insects and worms
LIFESPAN	Up to 11 years

ANIMAL FACTS

The nightingale's song has inspired poets and other artists over the centuries. The males sing most often during spring or summer, usually in the early morning or late evening. Sometimes the songs last well into the night. The song is meant to attract a mate. The songs vary in their notes and may include imitations of other bird calls. Nightingales usually live in dense woodland undergrowth and along streams in swampy thickets or hedges. When searching for food, the birds hop rapidly along the ground for a few moments and then stand motionless to listen for prey.

The songs of the nightingale have inspired many artists.

The nightingale is famous for the sad, beautiful songs the males sing at night. Nightingales spend the winter in Africa and return to Europe in the spring.

WHERE IN THE WORLD?

Found in much of Europe, extending into western Asia. The bird spends the winter in Africa, south of the Sahara.

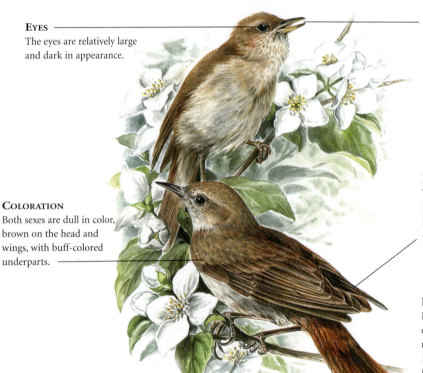

EYES
The eyes are relatively large and dark in appearance.

SONG
Only the male nightingale sings.

COLORATION
Both sexes are dull in color, brown on the head and wings, with buff-colored underparts.

RUFOUS TAIL
The rump and tail are reddish-brown, a color known as *rufous*. It is common to many birds.

READY TO FLY
Rapid development is essential, as young nightingales must fly 1,600 to 3,400 miles (2,500 to 5,500 kilometers) to their winter grounds.

TAKE A BOW
The male nightingale displays to a female by raising his tail feathers as he bows and droops his wings.

HOW BIG IS IT?

Northern Brown Kiwi

The name of these flightless birds comes from the Maori, the native people of New Zealand. The name describes the sound of the bird's call.

VITAL STATISTICS

WEIGHT	4.9–6.2 lb (2.2–2.8 kg); females larger
HEIGHT	Up to 16 in (40 cm) high
SEXUAL MATURITY	2–4 years
NUMBER OF EGGS	2, laid 3–4 weeks apart; may weigh up to 20 percent of the hen's body weight
INCUBATION PERIOD	75–90 days; fledging occurs at 4–6 weeks
DIET	Insects, worms, snails, eels; also seeds and fruit
LIFESPAN	20 years; up to 40 in captivity

WHERE IN THE WORLD?

Once found throughout the northern and southern islands, kiwis are now reduced to isolated pockets. Also present on smaller islands in New Zealand.

ANIMAL FACTS

Kiwis are usually active at night. They hunt using their keen sense of smell, which is unusual among birds. After smelling a worm in the soil, the kiwi plucks it up with its long bill. Kiwis had few *predators* (hunting animals) before the arrival of people, about 700 years ago. Today, foreign animals have spread throughout New Zealand, devastating native life. Kiwis are eaten by introduced cats, ermines, dogs, ferrets, and pigs. Few of the chicks survive to adulthood, and the species has become *endangered* (at risk of dying out).

The kiwi's bill curves down at the tip.

FEATHERING
The brown plumage is rough and shaggy in appearance, resembling bristly hairs.

LEGS
The legs are stocky, allowing the kiwi to walk easily. The bird's tiny wings are not visible beneath the body feathers.

TOES
Three of the toes are directed forward, splayed out at a broad angle.

NEST
Kiwis have a nesting *burrow* (underground shelter) dug into the soil.

NOSTRILS
Unlike other birds, kiwis have their nostrils at the tip of the long bill.

HOW BIG IS IT?

EGG SIZE
The female lays among the largest eggs relative to body size. It weighs as much as 20 percent of her body weight. Eggs are *incubated* (cared for) by the male.

Glossary

adaptation a characteristic of a living thing that makes it better able to survive and reproduce in its environment

amphibian one of a group of cold-blooded animals with a backbone and moist, smooth skin; many amphibians are born in the water and later live on land

aquatic plant a plant that grows or lives in water

burrow underground shelter in which some animals live

camouflage protective coloration that makes an animal difficult for a predator to see

canine teeth teeth present in both human beings and in other animals, used to bite or tear off pieces of food

carcass the remains of a dead animal

conifer tree tree with small, needlelike leaves that bear their seeds in cones; conifers are often called evergreens

deciduous tree tree that loses its leaves at a certain time each year and later grows new leaves

dingo a wild dog of Australia

ecosystem a group of animal and plant populations living together in the same environment and its *abiotic* (nonliving) environment, including climate, soil, water, air, nutrients, and energy

endangered a term used by conservationists to indicate that a species is in serious danger of dying out

eusocial a form of social organization among animals in which only one female and several males reproduce; the other members of the group care for the young

extinction the condition of no longer being in existence;

gland an organ that makes a particular substance that the body needs

grooming a behavior in which animals clean the fur or skin of other members of their group; it often involves picking off ticks and other parasites

habitat the kind of place in which an animal lives

herbivore an animal that eats only green plants

hibernation an inactive, sleep-like state that some animals enter during the winter

incisor teeth biting teeth, with a sharp, straight cutting edge

insectivore any animal that eats mainly insects

larva an early stage in the development of some animals, including insects, fish, and amphibians

marsupial a type of mammal that gives birth to tiny young that finish growing in the mother's pouch

metamorphosis a series of stages in the development of some animals from their immature form to adulthood

microbe a very small living thing; germ

migrate to move from place to place to avoid unfavorable changes in weather or food supply, or to take advantage of better living conditions

monotreme a type of mammal that gives birth by laying eggs; the echidna and the platypus are the only monotremes living today

musk a substance with a strong and lasting odor found in a special gland in some animals, including musk deer, mink, muskrats, and peccaries

nutrient any substance, such as food, that is nourishing and that promotes growth and good health

opposable thumb a thumb that can be placed opposite the fingers of the same hand; an opposable thumb helps an animal to grasp things

photosynthesis the way in which green plants make their own food from carbon dioxide and water with the aid of sunlight and a chemical called chlorophyll

placental mammal a type of mammal whose young grow inside the mother's body and are born live, including dogs, horses, whales, and human beings, among other animals

poaching fishing or hunting animals illegally

predator an animal that preys upon other animals

pupa an inactive stage in the development of some animals, particularly insects

queen the egg-laying female in a colony of ants, bees, termites, or wasps

quill long, sharp bristles of hairs that are *fused* (grown together), such as that of a porcupine or a hedgehog

roost the perch upon which such animals as bats and birds rest or sleep

scavenger an animal that feeds on the remains of other animals

species a kind of living thing; members of a species share many characteristics and are able to interbreed

stag a male deer that is completely grown

subspecies a subdivision of a species

temperate zones of the world located between the tropical and polar regions in which the climate is mild

territory an area within definite boundaries, such as a nesting ground, in which an animal lives and from which it keeps out others of its kind

threatened a term used by conservationists to indicate that a species is in danger of dying out

warren an area of ground filled with burrows and tunnels

wean to accustom a young animal to food other than its mother's milk

Resources

Books

Forest Explorer: A Life-Size Field Guide by Nic Bishop
(Scholastic Press, 2004)
This book contains guides and tips for exploring different
kinds of seasonal forests.

The Temperate Forest: A Web of Life by Philip Johansson
(Enslow Publishers, 2004)
Explore the plants and animals that live in temperate forest
biomes and learn how they interact with one another.

The Woods Scientist by Stephen R. Swinburne
and Susan C. Morse (Houghton Mifflin Co., 2002)
Animal tracker Susan Morse introduces readers to the plant
and animal life of American woodlands.

Websites

BBC Nature: Broadleaf and Mixed Forests
http://www.bbc.co.uk/nature/habitats/Temperate_broadleaf_
and_mixed_forests
Videos, articles, and images introduce readers to broadleaf and
mixed temperate forest habitats around the world.

EcoKids: Forests
http://www.ecokids.ca/pub/eco_info/topics/forests/
Learn about the trees that make up different types of forests,
the animals that live there, and the threats Earth's forests face at
this educational website.

Fantastic Forest
http://magma.nationalgeographic.com/ngexplorer/0201/
adventures/
Take a scavenger hunt through the forest at this website from
the National Geographic Society.

Acknowledgments

Cover photograph: Alamy (Horizon International
Images)

Illustrations: © Art-Tech

Photographs:

Dreamstime: 6 (J. Haviv), 9 (J. Feuxcosta), 28
(S. Ekernas), 32 (C. Taylor), 35 (C. Wei Wong),
38 (A. Huszti), 41 (V. Kirsanov), 43 (E. Gevaert)

FLPA: 10 (H. Lansdown), 11 (T. Whittaker),
25 (D. Middleton), 29 (D. Middleton), 33 (S. D. K.
Maslowski), 34 (T. Whittaker), 39 (M. Konig),
40 (N. Cattlin), 44 (R. Tidman), 45 (T. de Roy)

Fotolia: 16 (V. Zharoff)

iStock Photo: 36 (K. Hiki), 37 (E. Ferrari)

Masterfile: 22 (Minden Pictures), 23 (Minden Pictures)

Photos.com: 8, 12, 17, 18, 19, 20, 21, 26, 27, 31, 42

Stock.Xchng: 7 (A. Cerin), 24 (J. Soininen)

SuperStock: 14 (age fotostock)

U.S. Fish & Wildlife Services: 15, 30

Webshots: 13 (B. Brooker)

Index

A

American bison, 6
ant, 5; red wood, 39
armadillo, nine-banded, 30

B

badger, Eurasian, 16
bank vole, 24
barking deer. See Indian muntjac
bat, noctule, 29
bear, 35; brown, 22; grizzly, 23. See also
    giant panda
beetle: burying, 40; stag, 5, 41
bison: American, 6; European, 6
boar, wild, 12
brown bear, 22
brown kiwi, northern, 5, 45
buffalo, 6
burying beetle, 40

C

cancer, 32
cat, domestic, 14
collared peccary, 13
common dormouse, 25
common hedgehog, 51
common wombat, 36
conifer trees, 4

D

deciduous trees, 4
deer: roe, 7; Siberian musk, 11; sika, 9.
    See also European elk; Indian
    muntjac
devil, Tasmanian, 32
dormouse, common, 25

E

echidna, short-beaked, 37
ecosystems, 4
elk, European, 8
Eurasian badger, 16
Eurasian red squirrel, 26
European bison, 6
European elk, 8
European robin, 43
European wildcat, 14
eusocial insects, 39

F

fire salamander, 38

G

giant panda, 4, 21
gravedigging beetle. See burying beetle
grizzly bear, 23

H

hairy-nosed wombat, common, 36
hedgehog, common, 51
herbivores, 4

I

Indian muntjac, 10

J

javelina. See collared peccary

K

kangaroo, 34
kiwi, 5; northern brown, 5, 45
koala, 4, 35

M

manigordo. See ocelot
marsupials, 33-37
marten, pine, 19
monkey, rhesus, 28
monotremes, 47
moose, 8
mouse, 25
muntjac, Indian, 10
musk, 11, 13, 17
musk deer, Siberian, 11

N

nightingale, 44
nine-banded armadillo, 30
noctule bat, 29
North American porcupine, 27
northern brown kiwi, 5, 45
northern hairy-nosed wombat, 36
northern raccoon, 18

O

ocelot, 15
opossum, Virginia, 33

P

panda: giant, 4, 21; red, 20
peccary, collared, 13
photosynthesis, 4
pig, 12

pine marten, 19
porcupine, North American, 27
possum, 33
predators, 5

Q

quills, 27

R

raccoon, northern, 18
red panda, 20
red squirrel, Eurasian, 26
red wood ant, 39
rhesus monkey, 28
robin, European, 43
roe deer, 7

S

salamander, fire, 38
seasonal forests, 4-5
setts, 16
short-beaked echidna, 37
Siberian musk deer, 11
sika deer, 9
skunk, striped, 5, 17
spiny anteater. See short-beaked echidna
squirrel, 4; Eurasian red, 26
stag beetle, 5, 41
striped skunk, 5, 17

T

Tasmanian devil, 32
tit, willow, 42
troops, 28

V

Virginia opossum, 33
vole, bank, 24

W

wallaby, whiptail, 34
whiptail wallaby, 34
wild boar, 12
wildcat, 5; European, 14
willow tit, 42
wisent. See European bison
wombat: common, 36; northern hairy-
    nosed, 36
wood ant, red, 39